MW00953194

Southern Jewel

The Elements Within

By Ty A. Patterson

Amarylis,

There are some jewels that are so rare, so precious and so valuable that they are hardly seen, and maybe even unknown. But when you receive them you know their worth by the shine, the weight because of the substance, and cut, different from the norm.

Blog: meredithetc.com
facebook **Meredith** *Etc*
🐦 **Meredith***etc*

Meredith Etc
Jackson, Mississippi, USA

www.meredithetc.com (publisher's blog)

In the last hour, He gave me you.

Southern Jewel: The Elements Within

Copyright © September 4, 2014 Ty A. Patterson

All rights reserved.

Meredith *Etc.*, a small press
1052 Maria Court
Jackson, Mississippi 39204-5151

Keywords: Relationships, Mississippi, Poetry, College life, Family
6" x 9" (15.24 x 22.86 cm)
Black & White on White paper
Trade paperback binding
128 pages

Printed in the United States of America
Printed by CreateSpace
Published by Meredith *Etc*
Available on the World Wide Web as an eBook

2nd Printing

ISBN-13: 978-1500165048
ISBN-10: 1500165042

Visit Miss Patterson's author page online.
http://meredithetc.com/southern-jewel/

DEDICATION

To my beautiful mother, the late Victoria Patterson, who was my biggest critic and my loudest cheerleader. I finally understand her methods, and learned the importance of being versatile, and of embracing individual qualities rather than appearance. She taught me the joy of laughter, the power of love, and how to live out loud. Because of her, I am strong.

To my handsome father, Lucious, who teaches me, even now, the strength of silence, how to be self-sufficient, to cherish peace of mind, and that discipline has to be within or it will fade away. He taught me that what you do is more important than what you say. Because of him, I am wise.

TABLE OF CONTENTS

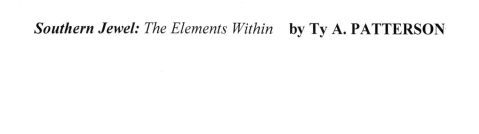

Southern Jewel: The Elements Within **by Ty A. PATTERSON**

Never had I imagined losing a mother… but I was blessed with a second one…

Ty A. Patterson

PREFACE

I grew up in rural Attala County, Mississippi. My parents provided us with a beautiful, simple life, but at some point I wanted something different. Children seldom stray too far from their upbringing. However, I walked on the other side of the tracks and evolved into a totally different person. Instead of learning from my failures, I became a product of them. But in the end, I returned to my roots.

Our youthful vulnerabilities cause us to surrender to the destructive influences around us. These periods in life can make us angry, sad, coldhearted, doubtful, and downright hopeless. But once it is in our past, we have the power to become strong, wise, confident, and discerning.

I learned the hard way about fake friends, crazy relationships, financial struggles, and how difficult it is to juggle work, school, family, a love life, a social life, and still try to keep the faith.

When I embraced my selfworth, I discovered the true me: a Southern Jewel, who like you, possesses the elements within: earth, fire, water, and air.

Read this book if you are searching for the best you.

By Ty A. Patterson

Meredith Etc proudly presents *Southern Jewel: The Elements Within* by Ty A. Patterson.

On one hand, Patterson's poetry describes error, drama, and carefree living, but it also depicts an evolution from youthfulness into maturity, and discusses friendships, romance, and other topics. Below is an excerpt of the poem *Real Woman, Real Man* in Chapter 1 *Earth*:

> All we want to do is be in our comfort zones. But even that is twisted. Some comfort zones include alcohol, drugs, gossip ... all because we use the excuse "only God can judge me" but we forget - one day HE WILL!

The poem *He Sent Me You* from Chapter 2 *Fire* eludes to the sensual essence of a man; an excerpt is as follows:

> Face to face when he breathes out, I purposely wait and breathe in just to inhale the most intoxicating fragrance I had ever indulged in. I wonder if he knows what shade of brown his eyes are... if you mixed black coffee, caramel, maybe brown sugar and my reflection... that's the color. I touch his hair and I feel as if I am touching the softest blends, feeling the most sensual patterns.

> God must really love me.

> He sent me you.

Southern Jewel is grouped into Then and Now intermediate sections followed by poems and letters which use the elements as metaphors to discuss diverse experiences. Enjoy it!

Advance Praise for *Southern Jewel: The Elements Within*

Ironically or purposefully, the first chapter of poet Ty A. Patterson's first book, "Southern Jewel: The Elements Within," is Earth. It alone has the power to bury the reader alive with conceit or excavate their soul with remorse. The choice is theirs to either embrace Patterson's empowering words of self-fulfillment or be damned to continue on a path of doom. The following three chapters – Fire, Water and Air – also help to quench one's thirst for acceptance of self and others. Good luck in trying to stop to catch your breath.

Alice Tisdale, Publisher, Jackson Advocate
http://www.jacksonadvocateonline.com/

Author Ty A. Patterson brings to the forefront the impact of living life first as a "Southern gurl (sp)," only to be developed into a fine jewel in the LORD'S timing. I'm sure that every reader will have a connect-to-life experience.

Iris L. Jones, Founder of Iris L Jones Ministries, Inc.
Iris L. Jones Enterprises, Inc.
www.irisljones.com - www.kmowinc.com

When Miss Patterson writes she does it from her soul. She shows her talent and tells some truths. This body of work will have you saying, "Yes!" "Say that!" and "I know that's right!"

Lynette Stafford, *The Magical Storybook Lady,*
Host and Executive Producer,
Off the Shelf, Greenville, Mississippi

This piece of art is Ty A. Patterson's soulful expression of poetic thought; she invites readers into her creative world which is open sharing the deepness of her elevated mind.

Reya Peach, Poet/Lyricist
Status Move

Miss Patterson's poem "He Is" embodies what I seek and need in a man. She hit the nail on the head with that one. High 5!!

Chearice Vaughn, International Model/Spokesperson
MSA Arts and Entertainment

EARTH

Earth: Vigor. Life has its ups and downs; some of our lows are self-inflicted, but learning from our faults thickens our skin. On the other hand, we can end up hardening our hearts and spending the rest of our lives mistreating others because we have been wronged. The messy, dirty times is the chaos in our lives. The earth in you is the strength that you develop as you overcome hardships.

Guess what? If it is in your past, you overcame it. It doesn't matter what happened. You seized it. You have earth within.

THEN

At some point, we have all looked at someone, shook our heads, and said, "They will never grow up." But sometimes, we need to look in the mirror. We don't always take responsibility for our actions, but there comes a time when we should push childish ways aside. We all know right from wrong, and when we know better, we should do better.

REAL MAN, REAL WOMAN

Do not let age define your maturity. There are people of various ages in the world, who have handled situations I could not imagine facing.

Teens have gotten jobs, taken care of families in the absence of their parents, and survived on whatever they could get.

Yet, the world is full of adults who take almost everything for granted.

Some of us cannot commit to jobs, friendships, marriages or ourselves. If you're going to be a friend, lover, parent, or whatever, do it right. And we wonder why the younger generation acts the way they do.

Who are their examples?

We dread going to work for fear of missing a party. We make sure we have an outfit for every occasion, but if people only knew what we were eating everyday.

Southern Jewel: *The Elements Within*   by Ty A. PATTERSON

We spend so much money to "have a life" but on Sunday we hesitate to give to Him who gave His life.

All we want to do is be in our comfort zones. But even that is twisted. Some comfort zones include alcohol, drugs, gossip, same-sex preferences... all because we use the excuse "only God can judge me" but we forget - one day HE WILL!

Good old school parents did not act the way we act. Half of us wanna' be our children's friends, and then we wonder why discipline does not work.

We may hang in crowds, do dirt with our friends, and mess up together, but nobody is at fault but us, when we simply choose to do the wrong things.

As an adult, look back at the things in your past you wish you could change, and make sure it never happens again. Then, look at the things that brought you joy and do your best to make everyday as wonderful.

If you know what I mean, then you are a real woman/man. Finally, surround yourself with people who are actually doing something with themselves.

If you cannot find anyone, then that should tell you something. Erase... and Replace.

Don't let anyone keep you from being positive.

And before you point your finger, make sure that you aren't the problem. Because most of us will read this and start thinking of other people these verses apply to instead of ourselves.

NOW

As a young single woman, partying, fine men, trendy clothes and traveling took precedent over my role as mother. I surrounded myself with other women like me. Which reminds of the old adage, *birds of a feather flock together*. We hired babysitters, mismanaged our funds, our time, and our priorities were misplaced. We were still single, and for years we were stuck in a cycle having beauty on the outside, living in complete emptiness, pockets and all.

THEN

The supernatural fictional character Wonder Woman was created during World War II. She symbolizes justice, love, peace, and sexual equality. But to me, women, particularly single mothers, carry the weight of the household without supernatural powers.

WONDER WOMAN

She cooks, she cleans... she gives her all.
Yet the things she does are looked at as "small."
She wipes tears, drown fears, and makes hearts smile,
yet those she gives an inch, always take a mile.
She loves, she hurts, and does it from her soul.
When God made her, she surely broke the mold.
She can treat you like royalty, but she still stands strong,
yet people close to her, often do her wrong.
She indulges in other's problems as if they are her own,
yet when she is in need, she is left alone.
She is envied, adored, admired, loved, and hated.
But she is the best thing God created.
She loves life and its trials,
even when her back is against the wall.
Yet people stand under her pedestal waiting for her to fall.
She shows every side of herself to those she holds dear,
yet they stray away due to their own fears.
Fear that maybe she is too good to be true.
Well, of course she is... but she made time for you.
As I sit here & wonder as to who this could be,
I see the "W" on MY chest.
Damn. Wonder Woman is me.

NOW

In the day and life of a single woman, there aren't enough hours in a day, and we need four hands instead of two. We are pulled in many directions, wear different hats, and still find something within us to give to others. When the sun goes down, and we managed everything that needed to be done with the resources within our means, we can celebrate being the wonderful women we are.

THEN

The wise saying, *"Everything that glitters ain't gold,"* is just as important, in terms of relationships, as the motto, *"You can't judge a book by the cover."*

PAPER OR PLASTIC

I hold back no words and I leave little mystery when I am faced with trying times and even more trying people.

Everyone has their moments and I chose to write instead of act on my emotion.

One thing you must do is stay encouraged when we have "heard it all before."

History repeats itself.

But if we know history has a possibility of making a swift return we should already be prepared to handle it.

In church today and through conversations I am reminded as long as we are alive, we will be mistreated, misled, misused, and misunderstood.

And guess what? We have to forgive.

Now, I have recently learned a valuable lesson in shopping.

We do not have to return to a bad situation, but we have to forgive and go our own way. Things happen for a reason.

If there is anything in this world you don't have right now, it may be that God sees how you handle the small things, and knows you are not ready for more.

If you want someone to love you right, but it doesn't seem to happen, then it may be because God knows you do not belong together. Either you don't deserve them, or they don't deserve you.

Think about how much we settle just to say we achieved something. We drive all around the world for bargains on food, clothes, gas, anything!

We know that we may be sacrificing value but what do we say? "It'll do...It'll work for now." Not realizing that the less time you spend looking for value, the more time you will spend making up for it.

The cheap gas messes your car up, the cheap clothes have strings hanging loose, and cheap food is unhealthy... now you are paying for it.

I tell you what. I am tired of the quick fix.

Yes, we want love, friendships, material possessions, we want to be "happy," or is it that we want to keep up with the traffic on the freeway?

My life is like SAKS FIFTH AVENUE, but I been letting KMART come in. Ladies and Gentlemen, some things just need to be left on the rack because it is on "clearance" for a reason.

That super-fine, educated, sweet man/woman that you swear should not be single... and you think you lucked up on a good deal....CLEARANCE!!!

There are some people that just cannot be helped. You cannot wish, hope, or pray a person changes just because you are investing in it.

When we try to make our own decisions without God's favor we ignore things we should use as a red flag (or shall I say RED-TAG).

Everyone has a history, and one's history makes them who they are. If they have never been around love then they may not know how to fully love you.

If they were never brought up in church, you cannot get them speaking in tongues unless you do it in a very ungodly way... know what I mean because it can be done, but I digress.

If they are spoiled because they were the baby, only child, or just a cute person, then, don't expect Bob-the-Builder or Dr. Phil when you need help with something.

Have your own resources and stick to your standards. Be your own person.

When you find yourself saying "It'll do" because you want things to seem better than they are, you are trying to get a discount. You can't do that with life.

You know why people are the way they are? Because

somewhere in their lives some bargaining was going on: abuse, no hugs, no church, bad language, bad habits, discouragement, manipulation, or just settling for whatever.

You do not want to struggle with a person who is carrying 20, 31, or 45 years of damage.

People can't change overnight. Whether we like it or not, a clearance item has no remorse when it malfunctions because it was purchased "AS IS."

There is always a reason for everything. You have to think of whether you want something valuable (you have to wait til' you can afford it) or if you want to get something quick and go through hell when it doesn't work right when you get it home.

I had some discounts but I tried to be slick. Some people don't care about the outside of anything, they just want a deal. But me, I like things that are presentable and still kinda' inexpensive. BIG MISTAKE. But guess what? The function and action matters as opposed to the physical appearance.

A person can say sweet things, be your best friend, and look good...you get that thing home AND YOU HAVE JUNK!!! What happened was that person marketed themselves to you, and BOOM, you got a deal.

Aaawww' yeah, you are on cloud nine because you think you found the perfect situation, friend, or mate and all along this person was like a dog in a shelter looking for someone to latch onto and share the fleas!

The decision you made was like finding money on the street... A MIRACLE (But full of germs).

Then we have the nerve to thank God for the "bargain" He had nothing to do with and doesn't approve of. God's choice may have been on the next aisle and we stopped on aisle three because we saw something that looked good and didn't seem like a risk...CLEARANCE!!!

I'm gonna let God do the shopping for me.

We are confused on what a deal is and what a con is. God may send us that person who may not have a Cadillac but he will put those roses down for you, do things for you without you asking, and treat you like a queen.

God will send a friend that may not have name brand clothes right now, but she will give her last for nothing in return. Your friends will not be eye balling your man, your friends don't have to dress like you or have certain possessions but they will love you and be happy for you instead of plotting against you.

A person may not look like they stepped off the cover of GQ/KING but he/she is gonna take care of you, listen to you, support you when you are right, and correct you when you are wrong.

It ain't about what you want sometimes. It's about what you need and as you live life, your needs will be #1 and turn into your deepest desires.

Be careful what you pay for. If you are a clearance item, don't try and sell yourself. Get yourself fixed, cleaned up, and mended so you will be of some value inside and out.

They don't need you. And you were only available because everyone knows how cheap and useless you were. CLEARANCE!!!

I could get mad at the bad deals that I have gotten, but it is my fault for not letting God shop for me. He created everything in this world, so, who do you think has better "product knowledge" God or us?

In life, things will not be perfect, and we will go through things daily, but remember history repeats itself.

So, will you be a valued customer at the dollar store of life? Or will you seek quality over quantity.

I could have all the friends and relationships I wanted, but at what price? That's just more friends that may fall by the wayside and more heartbreaks.

I cannot accept any more cheap items. I know you should be there for people and I will always do that. I compromise my true character for no one, knowing I cannot save people.

Some people do not care about themselves. So, how can they care about you? You know what their flaws are and you think if you take it home, you can patch it up, and create a wonderful "new" thing.

They can change...but they still need God to do it. Let them stay on the shelf. If you had waited on something worth more, you would not be picking up pieces of what tore apart in your hands.

I am beautiful, I am loved, I am strong, and I am not going to change because of an experience.

Wouldn't that be lowering my own value? Yes. No one should be powerful enough to alter you. God is doing my shopping for me from now on and I know He knows my style, my taste, and most important ...what I need.

By the way, some people know they are of no value and they will put themselves right in your path because they want to make you feel like they do: worthless.

They can get more from you than you can get from them and they won't apologize. They don't care. I'm glad God revealed the defects early before I became dependent and wasted time and ruled out all other options... just for that thang' to tear up on me down the road.

I'm telling you from experience, read the fine print, check customer reviews, and shop around before you call yourself getting a bargain or it will not last

NOW

Discernment, and being cautious can save headaches, pain and regret. Something may look good, but may be bad for you. But know, our time is too precious to waste on unhealthy and unfulfilling relationships.

THEN

Some people can find something negative to say about any and everything. They always talk about who shouldn't be married, who didn't deserve a promotion, why they can't stand so and so, what they wouldn't put up with in a relationship, and the list goes on. My all-time favorite was, "I just need to move and live somewhere else because nothing is here for me?" I want to reply, "Nothing will be new but your address."

YOU ARE MAKING MOVES,

BUT WHERE ARE YOU GOING?

This is not a "light bulb" moment, just a reality check for myself and whoever else that life is like an obstacle course.

As a military brat and a sucker to all these crazy reality shows, I have seen people use obstacle courses like "challenges."

There are different things to get through in life and there are different ways to go through it.

If there is a tire, u can't go under it. If there is a wall, you can't go around it. You catch my drift. The way you dealt with one thing, won't be the same way you can tackle the next. If you want to complete something, you can't be weak, and you can't depend on anyone do it for you.

I know at times we may feel like we are going in circles, looking down at our feet instead of up and out at the world.

We see what we want to see. If we opened our eyes, we could realize we are making circles in the middle of a four way stop. Find another direction or approach and just go. It's that simple.

If you are going through an obstacle course and you keep running into different challenges, that's fine. That's good because it means you are making progress toward a goal. At least you are moving.

The problem comes when you are stuck on the fence. You are not getting anywhere. Go get some training, and try again.

No, it's not easy, and no it's not always what you want to do, but you have to keep moving.

How many times have you run in circles and passed the sign that says: "Welcome to nowhere?"

Since my favorite number is three, I choose to see it like this. If I didn't reach a goal it's because:

#1. I did not do what it takes to get it or keep it.
#2. It was not in my best interest.
#3. It will be mine, when the time is right.

You may have your own way of looking at it. Now, I will say this, be careful putting your all toward something that has no value. We are old enough to know some things are pretty much bullshit and temporary.

Other things are just bad for you. You know what they are. I know what they are... moving on.

So, when I face some new shit, I can't help but smile. Because like the old challenges, the new things ahead test me. I love it.

I don't like to fail. Don't get falling and failing confused. We all can look at a lot of things in life we wanted and did not get. Not getting everything we want could be a blessing in disguise.

In all you do, be diligent. As for me, I am an obstacle course all by myself. I can be complicated, and I have been wronged by many, but they were left with mud on their faces, remorse in their hearts, and defeat in their eyes.

Don't just face challenges. Be a challenge.

If the "Welcome to Nowhere" sign is a regular landmark on your road trip please look around, notice the four way intersection and go!

For the ones who insist on cheating their way through that obstacle course you will always be a liar and a looser.

First of all, you may be skipping the very trial that makes you a true champion. And secondly, when you conquer things easily there is no work involved, and therefore there is no greatness.

Whatever your fears, weaknesses, issues, or habits were, focus on turning them from what they are, to what they were.

NOW

It doesn't matter if you take the scenic route, or travel in the fast lane, as long the trip is planned. There may be road blocks as you travel down the road, but there will always be a detour. Ultimately, staying on course will get you to your destination.

THEN

How many times have we made New Year's resolutions and did not keep them? We start thinking of new diets, new career paths, a new car, a new home, or even a new mate. The New Year always inspires us to set new goals. However, unless we make a plan to reach goals, setting them is not enough because we have no idea where to start, and how to get there.

NEW YEAR'S RESOLUTION

This has been a bittersweet year.
We have loved, we have lost, and shed so many tears.
Some tears were of joy, some were of despair, but never forget
God was always there.
I loved harder than I ever thought I would, and I reached many
goals I never thought I could.
I am sure if you looked back that may also describe you.
If not then next year what are you gonna do?
We saw the economy turn for the worse; we saw killings,
robbings, disease, and hurt in the land.
We also saw beautiful weddings, babies born, old boundaries
torn, & a Black President saying, "Yes we can!"
We know we must take the bitter with the sweet.
So, for the New Year shake that dust off your feet.
No more asking "Why this happened?"
Use trials as fire to learn from defeat.
Some relationships grew, some staggered, and some fell.
Don't let anyone use you. Your heart's not 4 sale.
Keep pushing in education, do your best in your career.
By being faithful your blessing is near.
Look at all you have. How did you treat it?
Some things in our lives, did we really need it?

Southern Jewel: *The Elements Within*   by Ty A. PATTERSON

Wipe your tears, erase your fears, and walk into what is divine.
Don't dwell on the uncertain that is left behind.
We learned lessons we should keep.
It's great to dream, but don't miss out because you're "sleep."
Life proved what was once high can be so low.
But what was once unheard of can steal the show.
Doing the same things, seeking different results is insane.
Yes, that problem still remains.
Treat this year like it's your first and last.
Do everything from your heart with no thought of the past.
If you need to let go, then quickly go ahead.
Raise things that give you hope from the dead!
Start over from day one with the same smile and desire.
Be positive and watch your life soar higher.
Admit and erase your mistakes.
We are born to forgive.
If it were not so, none of us could truly live.
Show your talents, God blessed us all with many.
Someone admires our gifts, and thinks they don't have any.
Be inspired. There is a purpose within us all.
The biggest setback in life is being afraid to fall.
Patience is a virtue but procrastination is a trap.
These different things often overlap.
The New Year is not for baggage there simply is no room.
You will be surprised at how junk changes destiny to doom.
Go for that job you want. Enroll in the classes and just pray.
God is with you. He will never stray.
Fall in love again, hold hands, and be true.
Keep your love right and don't worry what is said about you.
All you owe yourself is to do your very best.
With this year gone for good, you must decide what's next.

NOW

You never have to wait until January to challenge yourself because success doesn't have a start date and elevation doesn't expire. Sometimes, the best resolution might be changing your mindset. Leave the things that held you back in the past. When I truly began to make changes in my life, I realized we don't have to burn bridges, just stop crossing them.

THEN

It's easy to point our finger, but we can't blame others for our shortcomings because we are accountable for charting the path for our destiny.

**HOW CAN WE MOVE FORWARD,
AND WHO DO WE BLAME IF WE DON'T?**

When we think about change, are we looking for things around us to be different, or do we consider the fact that change may need to be internal?

When you decided that it is internal, are you giving up or moving on?

We make a big deal out of being a quitter, throwing in the towel, and having no patience. However, there is a time when patience is a curse rather than a virtue.

It depends on what we are "waiting on."

Personally, I have had the experience of speaking things into existence and there are times when that "magic" seemed to have lost its power.

When we don't get what we want, we often think something is wrong, instead of the fact that we are asking for the wrong things.

I am writing out of excitement because out of all the things I didn't get, I was blessed with things of more value and purpose.

Southern Jewel: *The Elements Within*   by Ty A. PATTERSON

I am happy disappointment did not injured my spirit, but it has taught me to appreciate what I have.

I look at my glass as half full instead of half empty.

Don't be depressed or waste a second of your time thinking about the person who won't come around, the mistakes that cannot be erased, the goals you have not reached yet, or any other petty thing in life.

Think about the people who have gone their whole lives blind, deaf, paralyzed, homeless, hungry, sick and survived.

The things that need to happen, you have time to make happen. The things that are causing you pain, you have time to overcome.

Don't worry about things you can't change. Change how you feel about them.

You can want people to like you, love you, or just be a better person all you want, but you cannot get so absorbed in wishful thinking that you lose sight of your own life.

When I look at myself, I can think of a million things I don't necessarily like, but there is someone who would die to have a portion of what I take for granted.

Let hopeless people and situations fade away so your purpose can get brighter.

It took me longer to accomplish things than it should have because I allowed so many situations to stop my progress.

We all do it and then we say, "Dang I am so-and-so years old and this thing ain't happened for me yet!"

There is a reason.

When we should have been setting goals and making plans, our precious time was spent in the wrong places, and on the wrong things.

I want too much and I "am" too much for this long journey. The same goes for you.

It's time to get there! And if you know me, you know I travel in stilettos.

No more stopping to take my shoes off!

If you cannot go with me to where I am going, move out of my way!

NOW

We have more to be thankful for than we acknowledge, and will reach greater heights than we can apprehend. Stumbling blocks should force us to climb, not foster reproach. Set standards for yourself and be a positive example to others, as you blaze your own path.

THEN

Why is it we wait until we hit rock bottom to call on the Lord? Jesus gets real popular during trial and tribulation season. And when we do pray we often forget to start with "Thank you." We start off making requests and asking why things are happening. When we are honest with ourselves and the choices we made, we will know the answer to the when and why questions.

WHY NOT ME

Okay I am a lil' overwhelmed right now from all different directions.

Sometimes I, and everyone around me, questions everything. Over and over we are asking Why not me? Where is mine? And when?

People are blessed because God favors them, and there are extra blessings in store for those who live right.

No two people have the same blessings.

From the outside looking in, it's easy to look at someone else's situation and be envious.

How many stars self-destruct? How many naturally beautiful celebrities ruin their bodies' tryna fix what ain't broken?

How many marriages do we really know about 100%?

Do we know what people in higher tax brackets really live like?

Southern Jewel: *The Elements Within*   by **Ty A. PATTERSON**

Different strokes for different folks.

We all have our views of pleasure, happiness, and joy.

Trust me they are not the same.

Pleasure is temporary and it can have you going against everything you stood for.

That's not happiness.

Happiness lasts a lil' longer.

Happiness comes from the great things in life like love, money, health, and fun.

But just as fast as you can be happy, you can be sad.

But joy is internal and nothing negative will ever give you joy.

Your spirit won't allow it, and joy is permanent!!!

Joy includes happiness and pleasure from things you can't touch or see like faith and hope, as well as the tangible.

We gotta seek more than pleasure, and even more than happiness to find joy.

Don't be too concerned with why we don't have something or someone.

As children of God, there is a child-proof cap on God's remedy for our lives.

We keep tryna' open that bottle knowing good and well:

#1 we will probably like the taste and overdose (greed)
#2 we may not like the taste and stop taking it (rejection)
#3 we won't even read the directions and take it when we get ready (disobedience)

I promise you I wonder sometimes why things don't happen for me like others, why the hoes are gettin' wived up, why "people-that-know-people" are making all the big bucks, or why I can't just make a YouTube video and get rich off a million hits.

I mean I could let a camera follow me around all day and become a reality personality.

But honestly you have to be lost not to realize that God is watching you so closely that he will move things of harm out of your way, yet we chase destruction.

He will put a blessing in your path, yet we step over it.
Of course by you, I mean us.

I can't tell you the answers to any of these when, where, and why questions, but I will say sometimes it's about simply finding you first.

There is a certain type of woman that men should be looking for. Same goes for us ladies.

Your brain is a better description of you, than your pretty face or your sexy shape.

Guys it's not your clothes, your car, your job, your looks, or your "package," cause' some "packages" should have "return to sender" or "damaged" on it.

It's important how you carry yourself.

How long you can hold a job or a friend, for that matter?

Check your mentality because it will eventually determine who you are.

Everyone doesn't wanna' hear you curse, cry or complain about things you let happen.

Everyone doesn't consider "gettin' drunk" a talent.

Everyone doesn't joke about everything to avoid serious issues.

Nor is everyone tryna' be too serious to have fun sometimes.

Find your balance.

I promise once you work on you, God will cure everything in your life from insecurity, jealousy, fear, bitterness, hate, hopelessness, immaturity, stress, pain, and despair.

While we are asking God, "Why not me?" He is asking us the same thing.

NOW

We often question our status in life. Most of us want to keep up with the Jones's, who may be riding good, smelling good, and looking good, but broke because they live above their means. We have to be patient because what is meant for one person, may not be meant for another. We are blessed differently, but constantly.

THEN

When we don't set boundaries for people upfront, it's hard to do it later. We can't afford to walk on egg shells around people. People are so afraid to standup for what they believe; they would rather keep the peace and let people do whatever they want as long as their inaction doesn't physically hurt people.

AND WHO ARE YOU?

I have somewhere to be in a few minutes but through conversations, listening to the radio talk shows, and of course life sometimes I think we know ourselves less than the people in our lives.

I'm sure this scenario is familiar: You are single by choice or by force, whatever the case may be.

Either you are looking while trying to remember you had a life before "him" or you stopped looking because your life was already fulfilled.

And here they come: the random people.

*They are either just someone who wants to be your buddy all of a sudden or someone of the opposite sex who wants to get to know you. *Rolls my eyes at the adventure ahead**

For whatever reason, you begin hanging around this person. Ladies are quick to call another chick their friend.

You turn into a lil' girl letting her borrow all your shit and forgetting to say what she can't borrow (like your money or your man).

Hhhmmm' your stuff comes up broke, stretched out, or you never get it back.

And what do you say? "Awww' it's cool."

Suddenly they forget how to drive (you are the chauffeur) and next thing you know you are carrying the friendship because this new chic is fun and likes to hang out and even though she needs a lot of work (everyone sees it but you) you gotta stick it out and be a good friend. Laugh Out Loud (LOL)! Ya'll kill me. Then when she gets on your nerves you wanna' talk about her and get on other peoples nerves about your issues.

So who are you?

Who are you that you cannot set standards in your own life and want to hand over the problem, which you allowed, to someone else?

Let's move on.

Then it's that person that wants to get to know you. They have no idea who you are, or that you were doing fine without them.

Or maybe they see it, and want to reap the benefit of you upgrading them.

Either way what do we do? We walk blindly into something head first, and when we begin to see the person isn't doing anything we can't do for ourselves, we make up reasons to keep the party going.

Never mind that all the questions that should have been asked were replaced with laughter.

Who are you?

There is nothing wrong with making someone work for you.

The same people work for a paycheck.

If they don't, you are really stepping into a mess.

Why can't they work for you? Labor ain't ever hurt anyone.

Stop acting like you don't know yourself.

It's better to be in your own company, than in the company of fools.

Stop saying God sent you someone you can't even understand or handle.

Stop letting people work part-time in your life and getting full-time benefits.

Who are they?

What have they done so good that you allow your life to be interrupted?

Now you have more altercations, more issues, more questions, more giving of yourself, and what do you have to show for it?

Having someone doesn't mean you can't still be lonely. Sometimes having someone is more work.

You find yourself going out of your way and that person on the other end will be sitting back riding high.

All the promises are broken.

You lose yourself and still don't know the person you are dealing with.

Like Maya Angelou cautioned us, "When people show you who they are, believe them."

I am very observant.

I, among many single mothers have done enough on my own to only want to include those that will help me.

Company is fine, but I can get that in a matter of seconds, along with anything else.

This goes for you too. Who is the person trying to get to know you?

What have they done for you lately (that you can't do for yourself)?

Having a man or having a buddy has never impressed me to a point that I expect less from either.

If you want to get to know me, you had damn well better already know yourself first.

It is better to be alone in peace, than among several people in misery.

God promised he will never leave you nor forsake u.

He has done more for you than anyone you will ever know.

Don't let people in your life who can't make it better.

Don't ask to be in someone's life that you can't contribute to either.

NOW

Strength comes when you rely on yourself.

THEN

What people say and do at times doesn't coincide. Words sound good but it stings when you realize people don't care what they tell you. Over and over I had to remind people of what they said versus what they did. It doesn't matter what people present to you. A lot of people talk the talk but don't walk the walk.

CAN YOU HEAR ME NOW?

"Do I say not as I do" is often said but it is not always true.

I have heard this several times. I know you've heard it too.

What if everything you ever did came back to haunt your life?

Would you even have that job, those friends, that husband, or that wife?

"I love you" are small words with meaning from the heart.

But if I asked you what it meant, you wouldn't know where to start.

Love is not "I tolerate you, I am comfortable with you, or I care."

Love is "No secrets, no lies, no worries, and no cries." If all failed, love would be there.

You cannot love someone in their faces, and downplay it when you feel free.

Southern Jewel: *The Elements Within*   by Ty A. PATTERSON

Be careful saying those three words, even a fool would agree.

Technology can help you say anything, but can put you on thin ice.

Afraid to show the ugly truth, so you disclose what's nice.

"Baby it's not what it looks like" means the opposite right off hand.

Why you start your lies with these words is hard to understand.

Some say believe none of what you hear and only half of what you see.

But if I have to play guessing games then "it is what it is" to me.

Truth is as clear as water. One drop of deceit makes it impure.

The slightest thought or gesture we make can simply mean we are unsure.

Friendship equals respect. And that respect should not be just for you.

No playing with fire, no untapped desire, and a friend respects me too.

"Just friends" is the icing on the cake - sounds sweet but you don't need too much.

How many homies' do you call, flirt with, visit, laugh with or touch?

You don't even have to answer because right now your thoughts may be rushing fast.

If I had friends, like you have "friends" how long do you think it will last?

I will end this with "I promise" because that phrase is taken lightly too.

Don't promise things that sound good because your actions will tell on you.

You can't control consequences, but you can control what you do and say.

Don't try to sugar coat the past or future, just be sincere each day.

Clichés are not all bad when you understand what they truly mean.

Until then just be honest and keep the slate clean.

No matter what phrase you blurt out, the truth with come to the light.

It will be revealed all the times you went left, while you swore you went right.

Don't feed anyone charming lies and think you're getting by.

When I can take no more, I'm out the door. No need to wonder why.

NOW

We all know that nobody is perfect, but there is a difference between mistakes and patterns. There will be times when people mess up and times when people just want to get over on you. Make sure you don't tell people things you don't mean, or make promises you don't intend to keep.

THEN

Believe it or not, some folks don't know how to treat people right. And others just don't want to. People don't always intend to make us feel bad, but they do. We have to be careful trusting people with our hearts, our life stories, our ideas, blessings, and even our desires. People who don't have good things going on in their lives, may have a hard time being happy for you.

WHEN TO SAY WHEN

You will be surprised at how people love to see you down, sad, or just want to steal your joy. No matter what you do for them or give them, the minute you find strength to decide to have a good day or a happy moment they want to take that away.

Not only is that selfish, but it is ungrateful, arrogant, and shallow for people to want to steal someone's joy. It isn't always an enemy so be careful who you think is in your life for the good.

I'm just glad to have God's hands on me. People will let you down, while you hold them up.

History repeats itself and the only thing that changes are the people. We are constantly going to church or seeking inspirational words to find truth.

Either you deal with situations, or you leave them behind. Those who are meant to help you will. Those who are meant to harm you will. Those who want to take from you will never give you anything in return.

Southern Jewel: *The Elements Within*   **by Ty A. PATTERSON**

That's just how it is.

Our problem is thinking bad things come from only bad people. Behind every face is a true purpose. Before you let anyone or their ways consume you, be strong in who you are.

Keep your values and instincts sharp. The minute you let someone make you believe something you know is wrong, you slowly lose yourself to that person.

If there are standards in your life you hold high, don't lower them. If there are things you want to stop doing, don't be around someone that does those things. If people aren't willing to do things you ask of them, even when they promise, it means lying to you is easy, and respecting you is hard.

Listen and pay attention to everything around you from what you experience daily to your dreams at night.

It's an old saying but, "Everything that glitters ain't gold."

Some people will come into your life knowing they have nothing to give you because they are still void from someone in their past.

When you find yourself working overtime mentally and physically to make things comfortable for someone, you best believe they are using that as fuel to conquer something else.

You could be feeding a monster, while your own spirit is dying of hunger.

There is nothing wrong with being good to those that deserve it, but if you drain yourself on foolishness, you will not be able or willing to be there for someone who needs you.

Many drained people have come into my life because they have given their all to the wrong person. The result is that they try to drain me. Don't lose yourself for anyone. Learn to let people go who are not worth the trouble. Know when to say when.

NOW

Be observant, stay focused, and evaluate your relationships. Sometimes friends and family encourage you the best way they know how. In other cases, people want you in their corner but you won't see them in yours. Make your progress a priority.

FIRE

FIRE: Passion! When heated situations come into our lives they may be about anger and or desire. What both have in common is intensity. Passionate situations can be exciting, but when we direct our flames in the wrong direction it can shift things off course, often destroying what could have lasted forever. We have to extinguish the actions and relationships in our lives that are negative and of no purpose. In the same token, we must find the things in our lives that are valuable and light it up! Have passion about your marriage, your children, and about those talents, skills, and gifts you have. When you have passion about making your dreams a reality, have passion about being in love, you have fire within.

THEN

Let's face it; certain people we know do the worst things and have the best life. They are like rabbits in the race. There may be some underhanded scheming going on, but they still seem mighty lucky! The truth is people plot and plan on how they can get things the wrong way because they don't have what it takes to earn it.

BIG GIRL DRAWS

There truly are not enough words to define what a woman is. Some seem to forget the essence of womanhood. I am so glad I was able to learn from the best.

Being a woman means being comfortable with who you are and not feeling like you need to prove yourself to anyone.

It means having a mind of your own and being able to accept the fact that you are responsible for what you allow into your mind and for your actions.

Being a woman is not about what you have or what you can get. Instead it is determined by what you desire and how you get it.

If you step back and take a look at your life, and you never once saw that someone wanted to be like you for a good reason, you have not become a good role model.

Furthermore, if sometimes you don't even want to be you, that says a lot. There is something wrong with the picture when you have to acquire things in someone else's name.

Blaming other people for your problem is just as bad as ignoring you have them.

A woman does not look for someone to carry her. If she handles herself the right way, she carries her own weight.

A woman should not offer her body as if it were the last supper. A man will chew it up, and spit it out, especially if it is nasty.

If the only time you are content is when someone is in the same sad boat that you are in, that is a problem.

If your joy comes from laughing at others or talking about people for no apparent reason, you should be ashamed of yourself.

What are you doing that makes you think you are immune to the same treatment?

A woman is a leader, not a follower. And if she is a follower, it is only behind those that can bring her up and help her become phenomenal.

A woman does not hide behind a smile in order to seem invincible. Instead, she embraces the obstacles and steps on them on her way to the top. A woman no longer plays games; she says what she means and means what she says.

For me, I didn't have a negative mother. I had a mother who would not accept foolishness from family or friends. She did not ride anyone's coat tails, yet she was loved and supported by everyone she met.

Even though I was 16 when she passed, the things she taught me are very vivid in my mind. I am everything she taught me to be. I am not the "damsel in distress" and I never want to be feeble minded.

Even if I have traveled down a road that wasn't meant for me, I had sense enough to leave a trail of bread crumbs to find my way back. Petty things are beneath me, but don't get me wrong, I will go toe to toe with anyone who thinks they can break my stride. If that makes you mad, tell God about it. Tell Him you disagree with His blessings, and although you had the same opportunity, you chose a different route.

Everyone has blessings in store for them because we are all equal in God's eyes, but when you think things should be handed to you whether you deserve it or not, you have missed the boat once again.

It matters not when little girls play, but when they enter the court they should play fair. If your mind is not of a woman, then believe me, you have already shown you need improvement in some shape, form, or fashion.

And while you keep thinking of a game plan, a woman would have scored, cut the lights off, and left the building.

NOW

Cheaters, schemers, and liars are going to be here forever. Realize some people are lazy and if something is going to be handed to them, they will take it. Don't be envious of dishonest people that seem to have it all. You don't know what kind of life they live. But one thing you must do is set your boundaries and me moral yourself.

THEN

How many times have we been damn near perfect for the wrong person? Things start out great but after the fireworks, we find ourselves tolerating deviant behavior. We try to be patient without jumping to conclusions. Pretty soon we find ourselves linked up with a person that we can't put a title on. We keep trying to work it out and stand by our man even though he is not committed.

NO RHYMES, NO POETRY, JUST REAL TALK

Everyday some woman is being shown sign after sign that she may need to end her relationship. Everyday man is figuring out ways to make his wrong seem smaller than it really is.

When we meet someone, we have the intentions of doing things differently, in order to avoid making the same mistake twice.

You and that guy have the best conversations about what you want in life, what you want from each other, and what you have to offer.

The truth is, more than likely, the guy is fronting, the girl is fronting, or they both are lying to sound like they got their heads on straight.

As for me, I am a lady going on 28 years old, who has been spoiled rotten and treated rotten, sometimes by the same person.

There is no reason for me to lie about what I want and expect out of life because my past has opened my eyes. I have learned to be productive financially, emotionally, spiritually, and socially in order to be a good mother, friend, or mate.

Sadly, there are some men out there who look at what you have to offer and decide to feed off you, as long as they can, just to fill a void in their own lives.

The truth is a woman is a precious jewel that should be treated accordingly. She should not seek a man, then spoil him, when it is better for him to do for himself. Remember, men can be like sponges.

Guys can soak up everything you give them without changing how they feel about you. They easily feel pressured, and if you squeeze some emotion from them, they will release you and everything you have given them.

Just like squeezing water from that sponge, they bounce right back in order for the next girl to pour themselves into him again.

Well, I am just drained. I mean literally just drained. Guys who conveniently let things go unspoken just to keep the peace and have the best of both worlds drain me.

They completely ignore what you need and want, and keep moving as if nothing is wrong. They hate conversations (after the first date) because how they really feel may come out.

Women can stay on the phone for hours, while guys always seem short. We have society thinking men just don't like to talk. A lie! They just like to talk about things that don't require any real emotion. Trust me, they gossip just like women.

It wouldn't take a month for a man to find out everything about you from the women around you; his buddies won't tell you anything, but you might find out something from his mom. Find out how he treats the woman that raised him, then you will find out what you are getting.

Lord forbid he ask you a question that he already knows the answer to, and you avoid it because it is irrelevant. He will go crazy. But when you ask him questions, you are being insecure.

For the first time, I am unable to defend man's actions.

No more giving him the benefit of the doubt.

Men quickly avoid the future with a woman and resort to friendship in order to keep us around. However, I have come to realize they don't know what it means to be just a real friend to the opposite sex.

The reason being is because they have it all twisted. Friendship should not be the result of a failed or fake relationship. A relationship is supposed to stem from a true friendship.

Ladies if you feel like you are the man of the situation, doing all the compromising, buying things, trying to plan dates, trying to take on his problems and you constantly feel you are not being treated like a queen, then he is not playing his role as a man.

Along the way some woman spoiled him to keep him and now he takes other women for granted.

Any Bible will tell you the roles of each gender. Men love the reality of being created first. They love knowing men are the head of the household and the superior gender. The real things some of them should be responsible for he doesn't want to do.

Now ask the woman who spoiled him, how a species of such strength became so weak?

"To whom much is given, much is required."

MEN, get on your job.

As much as we want to scream equality about doing things for men, they will never look at women with the same equality.

Southern Jewel: *The Elements Within*   by Ty A. PATTERSON

It is ok for women to change where she goes, who she hangs with, start paying for dates, meeting him at a restaurant instead of being picked up, she can "buy him things for a change" and she thinks this makes her a liberal contemporary I.N.D.E.P.E.N.D.E.N.T. woman.

NO! This means you don't mind proving to a man that you have his back. But, do not lose yourself trying to find something in a man that is not there.

If you find yourself hearing his apologies for the same mistake over and over, then he never was sorry in the place. He was just sorry he got caught, but not for whatever he did.

He is not going to up and try to show you anything. A pimp with many girls will always be a pimp. A hoe with many men will always be a hoe. Don't expect a dog to become prince charming.

He will let you know that you should accept him for who he is because the past females were so hung up on him they took the bullshit just to have him on their arm.

If a man has deceived you, led you on, withheld his feelings or just let you down, but tells you, you can be friends, he was never for you.

Sometimes we do too much for the men we care about, hoping for the same in return, but we can end up giving more than we receive. If you try to stop doing the things you did before, an insecure man may become jealous, angry and question your loyalty.

If they feel threatened, you can hang it up no matter what you have done for them.

Men say, "This is a man's world," but we must remind them, they wouldn't be nothin' without a woman or a girl.

We cannot even go in a store without saying "Oh he would like this..., I wanna' get him this...." and that same guy would rather get you drunk than ask you "Have you eaten today?"

Some women are quick to brag, "He bought me a drink." But she forgot she was drinkin' on an empty ass stomach.

Ladies, stop boasting about nonsense. Stop spoiling these men because they keep coming to me expecting the same thing. I didn't breast feed my child and I ain't finna' do it for a "man."

Manhood is not just a privilege, it is a must. And the perks should come with a price.

No man is going to cherish you if you keep making it easy. At the end of the day, you are creating the same stereotypical man you say is no good.

And please stop introducing guys you like or who like you to your desperate unfaithful friends.

Sometimes when a man doesn't like for you to be around too many girls, it ain't because he is jealous you have friends or wants to control you.

He knows your friends are messy. Hell, you know it too.

Females with a woman's body and a girl's mind are messy. That's just how it is. Men may not want you hanging with the messy hoes, but leave him in a room with them and he will fuck one as if you died yesterday. Underlying message - Men are messy too.

Keep mental notes on what so called friends do to other people because the only way to dodge their bullet is to leave their ass alone.

Women you get along with, are not necessarily your friends. We only get two or three true friends in our lifetime.

We often see what we want to see and we are quick to dive into something not knowing what it takes to stay afloat.

Know what you are getting into so you won't be crying later.

We may need to sit our ass at the edge of the pool and just put our feet in first. The only way to know him is to pay attention. Do not pick a fight if he does not tell you his life story. We all know Ike Turner and I will not be held responsible for your black eye.

Demand honesty and be honest. Better now than later. You can replace a man, but once your time is gone it is not coming back.

Don't waste time trying to change a man into the man of your dreams. All you are doing is creating a nightmare for the next woman.

If he is for you, you will never have to question it. He will show you on his own, everyday, without fail.

NOW

If you lose your dignity just to be with someone, or keep someone around, you're settling. People can abuse you by calling you out of your name even if they never lay a hand on you. But somehow we find that small percentage of good times and tell ourselves, "It's not that bad." Sometimes people want you to think light of their inadequacies so you will hang on to their smallest kind word or gesture. Stop getting pleasured and start being treasured.

THEN

I don't think we will ever stop using the word "haters." We all think somebody out there is hating on us. Most of the time, our closest associates are hating on us. If you hold them under a microscope, you'll find they are full of bad bacteria, jealousy germs, and bitch bugs. They are everywhere. You talk to them on the phone, sit by them at church, ride in the car with them, you visit each other's homes, and you see them daily at work.

STILL TRYING

It seems life is revealing a whole lot.
It has made me laugh because the things I knew were going to
happen are actually coming into play.
But to those living life to the fullest, give your haters some tips:
Please don't believe you have more purpose other than a laugh.
Please don't think your hostility and limited vocabulary is
impressive.
Please don't try to speak Biblically when you are a second away
from being a "hot ghetto mess."
Please just simply.....take notes.
Please don't focus on my life, your concern is not needed.
Please stop being "on the fence" thinking your presence is doing
any justice.
I do not need back up. I am an army of 1.
Please take all the things you secretly envy and apply them into
your existence.
Please make a "name" for yourself,
then no one will have to call you one.
Please believe you can't stop anyone.
....and YOU? You are still trying.

NOW

Let's go old school. Be down with OPP which means Opposition and Opportunity. Anytime you think someone doesn't want you to succeed, that is an Opportunity to defeat Opposition. What people think of you only matters if they are signing your check. It matters what your husband or wife thinks. It matters what your parents and children think. It matters what you think. Once we learn to surround ourselves with the right people, "haters" will be a thing of the past.

THEN

Our minds are the best diaries. Sometimes we can escape to our memories and enjoy them over and over again. A wonderful place to visit is passion. There is nothing like the fragrance, embrace, strength, smile, confidence, touch, or kiss of a man. We feel blessed, peaceful, and excited all at once; even if it doesn't last we still can remember the man that makes us melt knowing he is there.

HE SENT ME YOU

His radiance from a smile is brighter than the sun itself bright enough to melt everything down to my very soul; he walks toward me with the confidence of a Greek god; every step closer builds anxiety as if this was the first time I laid eyes on such a creation.

I have known him for so long, yet I still get butterflies as if he were a secret crush revealed. The embrace feels as if God chose to wrap me in the finest silk that was custom made to cover me from head to toe. To lay my head on his chest, my own heart dances to the beat of his. If this is a dream I am only hoping to stay unconscious for fear that all may be lost in reality.

He sent me you.

So many questions come to mind like why his voice is more beautiful at the earliest in the morning and at midnight deep & dark yet fascinating as if I were looking into space. Face to face when he breathes out, I purposely wait and breathe in just to inhale the most intoxicating fragrance I had ever indulged in.

I wonder if he knows what shade of brown his eyes are… if you mixed black coffee, caramel, maybe brown sugar and my reflection... that's the color. I touch his hair and I feel as if I am touching the softest blends, feeling the most sensual patterns.

God must really love me.

He sent me you.

Just to open my eyes and be so blessed to grace the earth with my presence and then to realize what is laying so peaceful, yet so masculine to the right of me. So beautiful, yet so rugged. Someone who gives me peace and contentment while at the same time makes me want to scream... even while he is asleep. His lips like magic wands... whenever he makes them move in my favor, miracles seem to happen. You ask me why I smile.

Look into my eyes and you will see. Without the slightest indiscretion attempted, it amazes me how hard it is to leave and begin my own day away from him. The most perfect thing about him is his flaws. He is human. He makes mistakes... and then he erases them... over and over and over again with his love and I can never seem to let anger take residence near the passion that has decided to dwell forever.

He is ruled by Mars and I am ruled by Venus a match like two puzzle pieces that are needed to complete a work of art. Sadly, the reality is that even forever has its end. At some point I must awake and tear myself away from what was and allow everything that has been captured in my soul to take me through life as if I am still floating. People think they know what love is. They have no idea.

God must really love me.

He sent me you.

NOW

A perfect love affair embodies the untouchable, flawless, passionate flames which takes a person to the height of erotic satisfaction.

THEN

When was the last time you had a long distance love with a person who makes it so exciting to hit the highway. You loved to finally get to see so and so because the chemistry, the connection, or the conversation was just long overdue. But in a split second it's time to head back home.

ACTION

It seems like forever. How long has it been?
I been watching the clock waitin' on the day to end.

Sittin' here thinking about the things we do.
You better be ready when I see you.

Step on the gas, cause' I'm headed home.
Meet me there, and yes I will be alone.

Bubbles in the bathtub, rose petals on the floor.
Wearing only a smile, I'll be waiting by the door.

Betta' than a movie every time you arrive.
To hell with Denzel, you're the sexiest man alive.

You'll forget Halle Berry, and be my #1 fan.
Monsters Ball was acting, and what she did, I can.

The height of the show happens when we collide.
I'll come where you take me, like Bonnie and Clyde.

Don't worry about rushing, I can handle the speed.
Run through my red lights. Love me with greed.

Damn, are you're working on an Oscar or Emmy?
Hmm! Well, I want more so what can you give me?

Southern Jewel: *The Elements Within*   **by Ty A. PATTERSON**

Okay, I'm a believer, you have proved yourself.
I know because, I can barely catch my breath.

This is the stuff I don't want to end.
That stellar performance that only you win.

Just let me lay here, and gaze upon your face.
You have me so high, thoughts all out of place.

In my heart I love you, but my mind lets you go.
Parting ways kills me, so I kiss you slow.

It is what it is. No strings attached, just passion.
My body is your stage. No wardrobe, just action.

NOW

Distance does build intensity, and time flies when you're having fun. Sometimes it's not about the future, but living in the moment. Escapes, creeps and rendezvous seem to be like a sweet snack - it's good when you get it, but it can only hold you over for so long, and then hunger strikes again.

THEN

There will be times when we hook up with people just because they are different. They bring out things in us we never tapped into. It makes us feel complete and almost as if they are showing us a new life. Even the arguments are sexy. Don't act like you don't remember being with that person that people swore was all wrong for you but something about your chemistry just sparked every time you were together.

OPPOSITES ATTRACT

I learned that no matter how many pieces a puzzle can break into, and no matter how different the pieces are, it matters when the beautiful finished picture is put together diligently.

Don't look at what your mate doesn't have. Look at what they have, how well you fit each other, and how incomplete you would be without them.

That scent that compliments you, would be all wrong on me.

It makes me laugh to see how simple things are in your four walls, everything in its place.

Not too much, not too little… but my four walls seem to be a party with changing scenes with every flick of the light switch.

Can we trade?

It seems as if my silence and happiness go hand in hand, yet when you have nothing to say, it's as if the world is coming to an end.

When you are at your best, not even Webster can outdo you with words, while I express my negative emotions verbally…

repeatedly. I know it's a headache!

Is it that you are the 'yang' to my 'yin' or the 'out to my 'in'?

Without you I lose, but with you I win... Damn.

Everything I see is the opposite of me, but like a puzzle it fits and how can this be?

Wouldn't it make sense if you liked what I liked, or if I shared your every belief?

I love the opposition and it keeps me on my feet...

Your taste seems so luxurious but mine is so ordinary... while I have never wanted for anything; your stories seem scary.

Maybe that's what it is. You are everything I am not. You wrap me in your arms under your beloved chilled air knowing I would rather be hot.

You are a trip.

You could watch a horror film without blinking, I could write a romance novel without thinking. You are a mover and a shaker, and I am a nurturer and a baker.

Maybe we need each other.

I laugh at the sight of my feet in your shoes. You've big feet, but small feet might give a woman the blues.

Give me your t-shirt, so I can inhale your cologne. Yea' I won't tell anyone what you have worn of mine, we are going to leave that alone.

You so wrong!

The scary thing is the farther apart we are, the better things seem to be. We get too comfortable at times. I get tired of you, and you get sick of me.

Do you agree?

I think it's supposed to be the other way around. It really doesn't matter as long as you are there, and I am not too far behind. With my tail and your head... damn.

I forgot... what was just said.

Don't wanna' say too much, but you definitely complete me, the things we do, I want to reveal, but Facebook might delete me.

Gotta censor my words.

You know what I'm trying to say! There is no me without you.

Through the highs and lows, there is neither ocean nor sky without blue.

NOW

Face it that person either brought you out or turned you out. All of a sudden what you didn't like, now you love. What you swore you would not do, you have now mastered. We aren't ready to get off the roller coaster ride, no matter what. The one you assume is too different, may be the very one you can't see yourself without.

Southern Jewel: The Elements Within   by **Ty A. PATTERSON**

THEN

Where are the suckers for love at first sight? That was definitely my weakness. There is just something about a new journey that gives us thrills. You know how it feels when you can't even describe a person anymore because there is just too much to appreciate and crave. Just when we have given up, out of nowhere, here he is.

HE IS

The memory of a "high school sweetheart" or first love

is embedded so deep, there is no one else I could think of.

Knowing when he speaks my heart has to listen

The one whose eyes always seem to sparkle and glisten

When he takes one step backwards, his aura, I begin to miss.

All the above is what he is.

His conversation may be unpredictable at times

Or just plain silence while trying to unwind.

Understanding, patience, compassion, and desire.

My wind, my water, my earth, my fire

All the elements flow through me with just one kiss.

Southern Jewel: *The Elements Within*   **by Ty A. PATTERSON**

Everything I can image is what he is.

Knowing his story, knowing his heart

When he is happy I smile, when he hurts, I'm torn apart.

His presence alone lets me know everything is okay.

His charm & sincerity has me speechless and I don't know what to say.

I can go on like this for days with a mile long list.

Everything I wished for is what he is.

Episodes from my past try to bring doubts.

I can't compare him to others, or situations he knows nothing about.

The ability to trust and let this man be a man

Erasing what others couldn't do and realizing what he can

Looking further than the outside, because the truth is this,

Whatever my soul ever sought for... he is.

The things I thought I would never get again

The innocence, the purity, and the connection within

Southern Jewel: The Elements Within   by Ty A. PATTERSON

His actions and his words going hand and hand

He is in control of his heart, and it takes his command.

No thoughtless mistakes, no ungratefulness, no greed

He knows a woman's worth. Every man should take heed.

You are the color of love, the shade of peace,

you are the texture of infatuation, you have the scent of a sea.

You sound like a miracle, you taste like magic.

If it seems unreal, just smile and know you have it.

I am thankful in advance for the happiness and bliss.

If you want to know who is making my world better - "He is."

NOW

A love like this is hard to find, when you have it, you have struck gold. The search is over!

THEN

Sometimes we can't move on because we want closure. We want people to apologize, explain everything they did and why, and listen to our side with no interruption. Sometimes we even want to start over and make things right. We want to cry together, give hugs, and hear the words, "I'm sorry." I held in a lot of feelings refusing to accept that everything would not end perfect for me; things may not end perfectly for you either.

NOT YOUR AVERAGE "DEAR JOHN"

Dear Past,

I am expressing these words in hopes of erasing you from my present. For sometime now I have ignored the affect that you have on me. While it is true you have taught me a lot, and given me limited happiness, not knowing the purpose of your existence played a role in my questioning the present and doubting the future. Without knowing it, I expected new things to have an expiration date just like you had.

Make no mistake, I do not want to revisit you. I take my lessons learned from you very seriously. But understanding you or wondering why you had to be MY past are the questions that will never be answered. You were once the present, you tried to determine how many times you could bombard your way into being in my future. But, you knew you couldn't last. To make a lasting impression you made it impossible for me to get clarity. You wanted me to constantly seek answers in vain because you knew that was the only way to stay relevant. The truth is you will always be the past.

One thing that is certain is the past has no control over the future. You can't stop the next day, the next smile, or the next source of love from coming. I know how valuable my presence is. I trust and believe it is a gift. My gift. While I applaud your scheme to make a lasting impression on me, I don't wish for anything to be different. I only want to make sure I do not expect the future to be anything like you. The dreams I hate having simply due to unresolved issues are not going to force me to seek answers.

I realize a true heart takes a long time to mend, and that a broken heart can only love halfheartedly. In essence, I was loved by my past, it was introduced temporarily to you, and therefore you could never be in my future. I cannot make the past my problem. There are some things I cannot fix. And yes, I tried, but I was fighting air. Meanwhile my present is here struggling to keep my trust, wanting my attention.

I resolved the issues from my past by accepting reality. In reality, you were meant to be my past and that is the role you will play for everyone you encounter. There is no need for me to wish you were different in your present form. I appreciated you for the moment, I believed you when you promised to be the future, but my eyes saw daily you could never be my present because you were never a gift.

Since you don't have the ability to change, I, the treasure you loved and lost, no longer have a desire to acknowledge you.

Thank you,

The Future Without You

NOW

Sincere apologies will never come from cowards. I accepted so many false apologies, when it came time for a real one, I forfeited that chance as well. When you revisit things your gut is telling you to avoid, you cancel your closure. People will push you to a cliff because you are walking backwards. They will just watch you fall. We have to start walking in the right direction so when we feel someone pushing us, we can see ahead, step to the side, and let them drop off instead. You may desire an explanation, but you don't need one.

WATER

WATER: Cleansing! The more we bury emotions, the more we intoxicate our souls. Find the humor in things, or admit you hurt. It's alright to cry. Let those tears wash away your troubles. The truth is you cannot always control a situation or people. Why not cleanse your mind? Thinking clearly helps you see better. Being calm helps you hear better. Thoughts can torment you; you can laugh about it and move on. Bathe yourself in emotions a little while. You have water within.

THEN

Everyone has that moment when they reflect on things they wish they could have done differently. If we could just get one more chance, we would do something else. It's not like we didn't have a chance to make better decisions. We just didn't. When we think about life do we really commit to changing the way we think, our conversations, our circle of friends, our ways, and goals? Or are we just throwing a pity party?

3:23 a.m.

I heard that life is like a drawing with no eraser.
It's like consumption of toxic reality with no chaser.
With every sweet moment passed, I long to ride in reverse.
I would put foolishness last and much more first.
Looking back on the path I was headed,
Never steering toward a journey I dreaded.
As time passes and I take life's classes, tryna' pick a major,
I gotta stop ignoring signs saying "Danger."
Like an artist drawing with only a pen,
how many mistakes can my canvas take before I reach the end?
Repentance is my white-out, strength is my paste.
A new start is amazing, and nothing I should waste.
It's ok to argue and cry if it seems there is no way out.
Learning how to tackle it, is what life is all about.
We don't have to revisit the past to make corrections.
Life comes with a choice of several directions.
Looking at all the times when I felt so high,
makes me start pushing forward instead of asking why.
So much in front of me inspired by my past,
my decisions, with precision yield joy that will last.
Can't compare me, nor share me, there's no category.

Southern Jewel: The Elements Within   **by Ty A. PATTERSON**

I want the best, nothing less in my life's story.

Spending days tryna' prove your worth to man, is like struggling up a hill saying you think you can, you think you can.

People dying two by two, regardless of who they are, makes me realize I have come too far.

Yeah' Matt's Shelter was once a home for me. Can't think you know my life based on what you see. I'm that 80% woman, yet you seek that extra twenty.

Not realizing that TY is what creates the word "plenty."
I got no eraser for my life and it shapes my heart, into this flawed, fierce, fortunate, phenomenal work of art.

A mother, a sister, a daughter, and aunt, lover, seeker, promise keeper. What more do you want? Even if I could go back in time and redirect destiny, I would make sure to still return as me.

NOW

As painful as it was, I accepted everything I went through because ignoring it didn't make it go away. I learned to adhere to the voice that tells me when to stop and when to go. Sometimes we have selective hearing and ignore that voice. We go ahead and do things and try not to think about it. When you chose to do wrong, you are really saying "At this moment I don't care about the consequences."

Southern Jewel: The Elements Within   **by Ty A. PATTERSON**

THEN

We can tell when people have love in their hearts because they always appear nicer, have more understanding, and the sun follows them. Now, either you are reading this and smiling, or you are rolling your eyes because love birds annoy you. It's not always easy to be happy for couples when you are single. You get tired of wasting time with the wrong people, being let down, and waiting on that special someone.

IT'S TIME FOR YOUR RETURN

You have been in and out my life, and I don't know your purpose or plan.

As long as I have known you, I have yet to understand.

It is so amazing when I have you but when you leave a part of me dies.

How is it you are strong enough to create laughter and also cries?

Will I ever have you again?

Are you really out of my world?

You are better than silver and gold, and diamonds and pearls.

Will I recognize you when you return?

How will I know it's you?

Southern Jewel: *The Elements Within*   by Ty A. **PATTERSON**

I don't want to take for granted the things you inspire me to do.

I wish I knew when I would have you back, cause' then I would have time to rehearse.

Ain't no shame in my game. I need you bad like a Jazmine Sullivan verse.

I got everybody wondering who I am talkin' bout,' some even think they know.

Some already have you, and the ones who don't shouldn't have let you go.

When you are around me nothing can take me off the "high."

When you are within me, I cannot explain how it feels or why.

All I know is you are universal. Everybody wants you, it's true.

But I have mixed feelings.

I have it all except for one thing: You.

I know I cannot seek you. Force you, I wouldn't dare.

I know for a fact I will have you again, so everyone else beware.

There are so many things about you that give me contentment, satisfaction, and a smile.

As I write, I am already excited because the wait for you is worthwhile.

All I can say is I am so sorry for whatever I did to make you leave.

There is no life without you.

I can't eat. Can't sleep. Can't breathe...

I had you once before, and I know how great you are.

People may not appreciate you, but please believe me in my show, you're the Star.

I could go on and on about the joy you bring, but I will let you take your time.

Just know that when I have you, things will be different. It will be so sublime.

No more wondering what I am seeking, just know it's from God above.

Does this treasure have a name you ask?

Yes, I'm simply waiting on ... "LOVE."

NOW

I realize now we don't need to wait on love because it will find us wherever we are. Real relationships are not hard. They just have hard times. What is the difference? The people, not the experiences, make the relationship. Don't equate being single with being lonely. Be patient and enjoy your wonderful self. Remember, relationships should not just be 50/50 because that means neither person is giving 100 percent. Love is all or nothing.

THEN

We make it hard getting to know someone new. We bring preconceived negative assumptions to the table. Love dwells where it can be free. It is better to have loved and lost, than to have never loved at all.

UNTITLED

They asked how I knew whether I had ever been in love. What is love? What is the difference between loving someone and being in love? The more I wondered, I found out I didn't know until the next experience came along. When you think you know, love reminds you the beauty lies within its complexity, and its freedom to be what it is. We often become blind, deaf, and dumb assuming people can do no wrong.

Love is patient; but in reality, the power of love is urgent. It is right now. Recognize love is being wise enough to embrace it with no judgment, fear, greed, or negative intentions. A man who cannot keep anything from his woman, is in love. To have someone rooted so deeply in your heart you can dream of them while being in their arms... is love.

When they are the first person you want to confide in, the last person you want to leave, the only person you want to need... this is love. To feel sick at the stomach if you cause anything but happiness in that person's life, and to hurt anytime they aren't smiling, is love.

Different opinions, literature, and experiences never really answer our questions. At the end of the day, if you have been through the very worse and you are able to love again, you have been in love and someone was in love with you. Many of us know what love is; but, we just misapply it. I want to be dominated by love. I want to be bound in love's chains. There i. no greater feeling than to feel someone was sent directly to you. I believe when you decide to submit to love, then and only then, will you be free.

Free from trying to say the right things and wearing what may appeal to the eye. Free from each other's past mistakes and growing in love. Free from the cosmetic surgery of failures: cheating, lies, and lust. Free from the corrective surgery of meaningless relationships, to repair something that started out pure and natural, only to wind up being fake and lifeless. Full of blasphemy like an overdose on Botox, looking in a mirror not recognizing your own reflection. Over and over injecting ourselves with things of no value, trying to maintain an image instead of letting nature take its course, and allowing love to make you over.

When I breathe in I can smell the cologne he wears, breathe in again, I smell his hair; breathe in again, I recognize the fragrance his own body makes from his excitement of me. I have been in love, and I would just as soon die if I could not experience this again. I refuse to lock my heart's doors even though they looked closed from a distance. I think you have been in love when you can remember being close to it. When you are not afraid to love, then you have been in love. When you hate being out of love, then you are in love.

NOW

I battled with whether I appreciated love or if it made a fool out of me. Sometimes, we meet the right people at the wrong time and vice versa. The most important lesson I learned was to simply make sure what I need is the same thing someone wants to give. When things are forced together that don't fit, ither bends or breaks. There can be no love without

THEN

There comes a time when we have no choice but to let lii happen. It's about seeing how strong we really are. I get tired o trials just like you do. But, we have to remain positive and use our situations as a way of finding the alternate route. There is always a detour that takes you exactly where you need to be.

RANDOM

I have no script. I just want to write.

I had a lot of things going on lately. I often think back at how much I had on my plate and how someone would always say "Ty you are doing a great job, you deserve more, you are such a great person, I love you to death blah' blah' blah'..." and these words sound great. Not to mention they were partially true.

But, I realized that the same person(s) giving me the lip service were the same ones basically sitting around watching me struggle. They did absolutely nothing to help me, nothing to show me their appreciation (words only go so far), and mainly did everything but kill me mentally, while smiling in my face, wasting my time, and constantly asking me for things, but never once giving.

I don't know where the time and energy came from, but I gave it constantly.

I have seen so many people complain, mope, cry, converse (over & over), curse people out, and change their whole demeanor because things didn't go their way.

*ngry. That's perfectly normal. But, how can you lead
a dead end, never get a clue to turn around and back
ur car run out of gas there and then "bitch" because
no idea how to get home?*

*:h as I hate going through bad times, I will be perfectly
t and say there are huge blessings and lessons at the end
ery trial. People often say I make excuses for others simply
ause I recognize my own role in situations, and I admit the
rt I played may have been wrong. I don't put all the blame on
nyone even when I think they deserve it. I choose to accept my
;hortcomings because I have to learn from them.*

*I cannot begin to tell you the things I have gone through even
within the past 3 months. I won't even go back 3 weeks.*

Do I think I did something wrong to deserve those things? Nope.

*Do I think there are things I could have done to avoid them?
Definitely.*

*I already see the doors opening for me in different directions. I
see why certain things happened, and I realize it was 100% for
my good. What I think is good, is nothing compared to the great
things God has in store for me.*

*I normally handle things in my life. I fix things. I make things
right. I was the "mother" of all my circumstances. But it was the
"father" who let me know how it can go down, when I didn't
know my role. He is always in control.*

We don't have to wonder about a thing. All we have to do is take heed to any voice we hear telling us to go the other way. Once we learn to lean not unto our own understanding, we will not worry about who is there for us, who means well, who is sincere, and who is meant to be in our lives.

Never say "God didn't answer my prayer." He answers every single one of them with a "yes" or "no." Please accept the fact that "no" is an answer! It's just not the one we like.

In due time, you will love and appreciate all the "no" answers God gives us and realize why. It is His way of saying, "This ain't what you need."

Be patient, be diligent in your purpose, and trust what God has for you is for you. But, if you don't recognize it, and act carelessly; someone else may receive it.

As for those trials in your life, please stop blaming others. You let them happen. Stop finding fault with everyone around you (people you don't even know) just because you can't get the courage to stand up, even if it means standing alone.

You don't need someone to tell you what you deserve because the same people that can talk to you, can talk about you.

Know for yourself what is best and go that route. God gives us all one tank of gas, once it's out, it's out, and you never wanna' run out of gas on a dead end road.

NOW

Where would we be if we stopped everything we started? What if we refused to get over anything or anyone? What if we knew what we wanted, but never made an effort to get it? Some things take time to get over, but if you don't pick yourself up you will never move forward. During our school days, we knew we had all year to get it right. But if you didn't take responsibility for your assignments, you would repeat the class. Life is the same way and it doesn't get easier. Life doesn't care who distracts you along the way. You have to keep it moving.

THEN

Who still gets love letters? Better yet who writes them? I can't really appreciate emails and texts as much as a letter. When someone wrote a letter, it took thought, it took time, and it had meaning. A love letter is special. I use to save love letters, and I paid attention to everything from how he crossed his t's and dotted his i's, to the cute way his writing went from cursive to print, and back to cursive. The written art in the letter meant he was trying to make it pretty for me.

MY LOVE LETTER

My love,

I haven't written one of these in some years - maybe since high school. So I decided to write you before I explode. Man, where do I begin? When I first met you, I had no idea what I was in for. I was determined I had no time or desire to meet anyone. I was only going to stay "focused" and "do me." LOL!

I didn't want to go through the preliminary steps of learning someone's likes, favorite colors, favorite foods, hidden talents, and things I should be aware of. That takes too much time and you still end up with a different person than you thought you had. Until I decided on you. From making me laugh, to making me cry, I fell in love.

I think you were already there, and simply waiting on me to get there with you.

You are truly the man of my dreams. Because you are not perfect, but you seek nothing less than perfection which is why you found me. You match me. You know me. You love me. I can share anything with you: heartache, prayer, laughter, disagreement, money, love, trust... and you give it back double. How come you are so wonderful? Why are you so genuine? I am beyond lucky. I am blessed.

You will never stop being my superman and for that, just like a shadow, I will always be there. My family loves you, my friends like you... and I really feel like this was a part of a greater plan. We will be that power couple. Because we both realize that God is love. He put us together and I look forward to every chapter you are creating in my life. I am enjoying just turning the pages with you. If I make errors in this letter then my bad... you know what I mean anyway. You are my best friend and the next step we take will always lead to a higher place. I love you and I will call you later.

2 hearts
+ 2 gether
4 ever

NOW

Sometimes you can meet someone who makes you want to write about your feelings for them because you can't really tell them how you feel. A card won't always get it just right. A letter is from the heart and requires more thought than our beloved texts, tweets, and emails.

THEN

When it rains it pours, and sometimes the storm seems to never end; but it will.

YOU THINK YOU KNOW

Don't be fooled from my smile and laughter. It doesn't mean I'm alright.

Uncertainty is getting the best of me. Deep down, I'm losing the fight.

What more can I bare in this world?

What does my future hold?

The storms of life are raging.

I'm drowning, truth be told.

Prayer will help in most cases, but I control my own fate.

I wish I could forecast the outcome, before it is too late.

I'm starting to question my existence, my lows are so unreal.

One problem after another, everything tumbling downhill.

If I close out the world I'm selfish, yet being open causes pain.

When bad days outweigh the good, then what the hell do I gain?

Can't keep pretenders for no reason, I would rather step back.

Where they are headed, I can't go. I can't be a wolf in their pack.

Southern Jewel: The Elements Within   **by Ty A. PATTERSON**

Making choices today that will haunt them, living for quick delight

Crossing lines that lead straight to hell on a blazing first class flight

Should I shun love if it is not perfect, or wait for the rose to bloom?

What if the precious rose withers because the sun has left the room?

My eyes & ears should help me, but lately they make matters worse.

I wonder how close love is from being a blessing to a curse.

What relationship doesn't have issues?

What building has no flaws?

When broken down to the foundation, you will find the cause.

If you don't mean well you can't be here. Disloyalty must depart.

The worse thing to do to someone close, is break their sincere heart.

It's not for me to make all the effort, while others do the least.

I know I am a beauty, but I can also be a beast.

Words are like a pencil, they can be erased, but you know it was there.

Southern Jewel: *The Elements Within*   **by Ty A. PATTERSON**

Actions are like ink. No eraser. The marks left behind go nowhere.

They say if you're meant for greatness the devil lives at your door.

Well, he must have a key to my house. He is closer than ever before.

His tricks can't make me a weak link.

If I am not first, then I am last.

I vow to be an overcomer, with depression a thing of the past.

NOW

There is always a beautiful, remarkable rainbow at the end of every storm.

THEN

Being a mother is a sweet, challenging, and rewarding privilege. However, sometimes we focus on what the father is doing or not doing, more than ourselves and the baby. I did not feel like being the mother and father, because my baby deserved both. I battled with the thought of termination and even adoption. Sometimes, we make conscious decisions about intimacy, without thinking of the consequences.

NO TIME FOR "TY"

Eyes burning from lack of sleep, all my baby does is weep.

Where is peaceful rest and sweet dreams? Nothing lately has been what it seems.

"I promise you this, I promise you that," I have too many roles and can't wear one more hat.

No time for Ty when I am barely able to move.

Thinking I found a winner yet always seeming to lose.

Apologize for being fed up, be sorry for what I didn't cause?

Hide myself to protect your ego, love yo' dirty draws?

Nah' I'm busy taking care of business and things along life's way.

No time to seek revenge, you'll get yours one day.

Southern Jewel: *The Elements Within*   by Ty A. PATTERSO

As you push everything to the side that isn't on your list,
have fun on your way to the top cause' God will handle this.

I will get my quality time no more doing what you think is best.

Using my eyes to see past the surface, but I could care less.

Taken for granted while you cherish nightmares from your past.

Can't let go to make a good thing last.

Everyone else coming before Ty, and you have no explanation of why.

You made your choices and what will always be first to you.

Life isn't about what you say, but more so what you do.

I have my "picks and chooses" involving all I claim to love.

But I vow to give myself the spotlight and that will be enough.

NOW

Men you have to be strong, and be there for your children and family. On the other hand, if one parent is not there, the other has to love and accept the responsibility of being both, as difficult as this task is. Although the relationship is not going the way it should, when you neglect the mother you neglect the children. I have a secret. Women like to be strong just like men. They may not always tell you how much they need you. Maybe they don't feel that you deserve to hear it. Men are needed and wanted in the lives of their children. If things don't work out in

onship, your children will love you the same because
ng to them. Take pride in being a father regardless of
what any woman thinks about you.

AIR

AIR: Life! Many of us forget about air because we cannot see it. We certainly can't see God. But just like air, He is everywhere. If it were not so, we would not survive. Every miracle or blessing, whether unexpected or intended, is of God. He is the air we breathe. Inhale the goodness of life by overcoming your obstacles, nurturing healthy relationships, showing compassion for others, and following your dreams. When you breathe in God's grace, you have air within.

THEN

We will never know what we can accomplish if we lack confidence. God gives everybody talents, but it takes other people to remind us. It became clear to me it wasn't always about meeting the right person, but about becoming the right person. Believing you are worthy of excellence, will set the stage for victory.

FAITH

The best feeling one can have is faith in what you cannot see.

Seeing things that are not, as though they were and knowing what is not, can be.

No matter how much I try, I cannot help but smile and be overjoyed.

God breathed life in what the enemy thought he destroyed.

I sing because I am happy. I sing because I am free.

I sing because what God has for me, it is for me.

I tried to take short cuts, and I kept making the same mistakes.

I see so many great things in store. I cannot stop trying no matter what it takes.

My heart is light. My worries are few.

No longer can I think about things I have been through. I don't

Southern Jewel: *The Elements Within*   **by Ty A. PATTERSON**

want my life to be a blank page. I want it to be a testimony.

As long as I love unconditionally, God promised to never leave me lonely.

He is blessing me every day. And I am loving every second, minute, and hour.

It's only because I stopped fighting His battle, and recognized His almighty power.

For those of you who have helped me in any way great or small, you were there when my back was against the wall.

I have so much respect for you, even if all you did was make me laugh & smile.

Little do you know, everything you do is worthwhile.

True enough things could be different, but there is nothing I can do but move on.

Often times what we call right, turns out to be all wrong.

I appreciate trials and stumbling blocks. Even those which are present today.

It's not just words you have heard, God will "make a way."

NOW

I would love to say as long as you have faith, the sun will always shine in your life, but it won't. As stated in 2 Corinthians 5:7, "We live by faith, not by sight." The rain in your life is for a reason which allows you to grow. After the storm, the sun shines at its brightest. Just like those rays of sunshine, faith dries doubt and presents a new start, full of promise.

THEN

There is nothing like a true friend.

BOOMERANG

You are wiping my eyes before a tear had a chance to fall.

Though, I had a ton of sad stories, you listened to them all.

Years keep passing, yet you remain the same.

Time seems to stand still at the mention of your name.

What is it that keeps you near me, what is the mystery?

Is it the fact that it's not an act, but just pure chemistry?

Nothing about you changes, your eyes, your warmth, your smile.

Now you are the definition of swagger, and man I love your style.

Just to be around you, if we never say a word, something fills the air like roses with a melody unheard.

You've always been there for me, you let nothing keep you away.

Even when I am down, you come around & you make smiles come to stay.

You always make your way back to me after all is said & done. Many have tried to top you. But how many succeeded? ... None.

Thanks for finding me once again; this time it's all about you.

The place I'm giving you in my life is long, long overdue.

It's a beautiful thing to find devotion, what a blessing to find this gift.

Though I may not see you all the time, I think of you and my soul starts to lift.

For every door that has closed, you seem to have the key.

I am so glad you never left, you were always there for me.

NOW

When we feel alone we can find comfort in friendship. Being able to lean and depend on someone genuine is precious. God is the very best friend we could ever have. Hebrews 13:5 says "He will never leave you, nor forsake you."

THEN

Sometimes it seems we are a target. Often when one bad thing happens, there is another, and another, and another. This is the domino or snowball effect. Back to back things go from bad to worse and we don't want to hear any encouraging words. We just want to see better days.

SMILE

Some things never get old. When joyful thoughts I hold dear, seem to fade away like a sunset over a horizon, I remember them again and everything becomes clear and the sun rises in me.

Thank God for reflection.

I admit I replay old memories I would rather forget, faces I wish I had never met, and things I never wanted to go through. But why torture myself when life goes on? Why dwell on things that have no regard for me?

Nahhh' time waits for no man. I just feel like smiling instead.

Some things never get old. Like all the "first times" we can never erase. From childhood on up... first applause for something I did, first awards, first time traveling to certain places, first dates, first kiss, and my first born. The list goes on.

Those are the thoughts I want for my daily bread. Of all days, today tried to be the worse. By 8:15 a.m. I was ready to throw my hands up in the air and say forget it. Nobody knows my story, nobody knows how to handle me, and nobody knows how to be there.

But, I always end up with a song in my heat because I refuse to be defeated. I have a responsibility to act like I am blessed! There are too many negative people out there and there is no room for another one. People may disappoint me, I won't disappoint myself. And just like that, my favorite memories rush into my head like a flood. My thoughts, my fatigue, my broken heart, and my disturbance is submerged in peace.

Some things never get old. Being rescued is one of them. God has rescued me continuously, sometimes from myself. Now I trust when I am led to a cliff, I will either land on my feet or learn to fly. There is no time to waste, feeling defeated.

Nahhh' time waits for no man. I just feel like smiling instead.

NOW

I had to not only look at what I overcame, but thank God for guiding me. We do not have to wear our trials on our faces because someone out there just needs a smile from us. The world needs us to remain strong. Perseverance can give us unmatched happiness. Psalm 30:5 says "Weeping may endure for a night, but joy comes in the morning."

THEN

When we can't change a situation we often feel better when we can pull something good from it. The hard part about it is hanging on to that "shoulda' coulda' woulda'" mentality. Nothing external lasts forever, but time goes on without ceasing. Instead of pondering over those bad days and relationships, let them go so you can see the reason behind it all.

THE BEST AND THE WORST OF DAYS

The worse thing about the best days of life is no matter what, it ends.

All my firsts, my once in a lifetimes, my bests, and my wins.

What I wouldn't do to stay on cloud nine forever and kiss the sky. But knowing it's impossible, I kissed the past goodbye.

Is this a good thing or a bad thing? I must make room for better days to come.

Out of all the things I had and lost, I would only reach back for one.

I would take with me the best days of love, the smiles, and carefree times.

I would take the sweetest words I had ever heard and even the cutest lines.

I could care less about things I have, the recognition, the rewards, if I could live everyday in love and contentment

Southern Jewel: *The Elements Within*   **by Ty A. PATTERSON**

because the battle is the Lords.

But, since I cannot be the bag lady and carry anything weighing me down, I have decided to be weightless and empty my past so new love can be found.

Bitter-sweet and teary eyed I can only be glad, and be thankful for love God gives daily, and the soul mate I once had.

Outsiders don't understand; they have their own views, but misery loves company, and they couldn't walk a mile in my shoes.

The silver lining around this cloud is maybe one day I will love again.

Who it will be? Only God can see… and send me a new best friend.

Smiling through tears of confusion about things I cannot control, only shows I was sincere, and I definitely played my role.

Whether this is goodbye or see you late, a new start for me begins.

The best thing about the worst days of life is no matter what, it ends.

NOW

Ecclesiastes 3:1 says "To everything there is a season, and a time to every purpose under the heaven." Carrying the past around with us, forces us to deal with things that are no longer relevant. I have thought about situations with people that they aren't even thinking about anymore. Not only do grudges stunt the growth of relationships, it burdens your mind. Dwelling on the negatives in our past will define us.

THEN

At some point, whether we want to admit it or not, we have envied someone else's life. I saw people with gorgeous spouses, nice houses, pretty hair, perfect shapes, flawless skin, awesome jobs, and even their friends looked perfect. You know how we start comparing our reflections to others. You wonder why God made you look a certain way, be born to a certain way of life, or have certain experiences. Sometimes want more than we have.

ALL I NEED

Every time I think there is no way up or no way out, God proves what "staying in His will" is all about.

Never had I imagined losing a mother; this is true, but I was blessed with a second one and a beautiful sister too.

Never could I see myself past a college degree, a Master's later, now I am seeking a Ph.D.

There are times when love has proved to be unreal, but I refuse to be bruised, and I declare all my wounds healed.

Then, there are days when it seems that blessings overflow.

All I can do is thank God, because He is my high for every low.

Who would have thought, I would bring life into this world, and even have what I wanted - a beautiful baby girl.

No her father isn't around, but that can't stop my life. Someday a man will be her dad, and I will be his wife.

Southern Jewel: *The Elements Within*   **by Ty A. PATTERSON**

As for now, I'm just thankful. Even when I want to complain.

Out of all who chose to walk away, the ones who count remain.

I know how it feels not to have things and yes I know its hurts,
but not have anything in your heart is much worse.

When you see me physically, don't put me in a category.

You will never ever, know me, until you know my story.

Hard work, chump change, deceit, and tears have put dents in
my heart.

But what really made an impact on me is having hope from the
start.

I may not be what you think is "ideal" and that's alright with
me.

I am blessed for the smallest things, and grateful I will always
be.

For everyday my eyes have seen and for every smile I had,
I looked back, recalled bad days, rejoice, and I am still glad.

I'm happy because I choose to be, I love hard because I must.

And no matter how my past went down, I still have trust.

I pray you stay encouraged, and never feel defeated.
In all you do, treat others how you want to be treated.

The things that seem in good fun will someday come to an end.

God tells us there is no difference in wrong doing. A sin is sin.

I trust what, will be, will be. I trust God will make a way.

Patience is worth having to bring me out of my yesterday.

NOW

Every person on earth is loved and cherished by God no matter what they have done, how they look, how they talk, or what habits they can't seem to break. Take comfort in knowing agape love exists. Matthew 6:33 says, "But seek ye first the kingdom of God, and his righteousness; and all these things shall be added unto you."

THEN

God has a calling on our lives, but we must change how we think, act, and live. Instead of changing, we carry doubt. What if we do all we can, and still seem to hit rock bottom? What if we are meticulous, and still get caught up? What if we give at church every Sunday, yet live check to check? In the end, we want change, fast.

MY QUESTIONS ALREADY ANSWERED

What is it you are trying to show me?

Trust me I'm dying to know.

Is it wise to take things into my own hands, or is it best to let things go?

Everything and everyone seems to be misleading. One thing contradicts the next.

I need to know the path for my future. I need you to keep me in check.

Life is supposed to be a blank canvas, carefree, with no worries for what is to come.

Tell me why good people finish last, while the foolish have all the fun?

What is it you are keeping from me?

Am I going the wrong way?

I promise you I will take heed to your answer and in your will I shall stay.

It's hard trying to figure this out. Plus, it's taking up a lot of my time, and I can't help thinking you showed me once, but I was too blind.

I have walked in storms with nothing over my head letting rain fall where it may.

The water is getting high. I feel myself getting carried away.

I will be more aware of things I hear, and more observant of things I see.

All I ask from here on out is for you to show the truth to me.

I will wait for what is in store. I won't be swayed by the "too good to be true."

I will let everyone around me keep spinning their wheels because I am waiting on you.

Sure it will feel at times as if things are passing me by.

I don't want to go back to doing things my way, only later to ask why?

I take it as a compliment you try hard to shield me from pain, even when I forget I can't swim and go stepping back out in that rain.

With a smile I can say you made me different, I couldn't act like another person if I tried.

Whoever told the world I was a typical girl, I know now they have lied.

I still don't know where I am headed, because the future I cannot tell.

I understand why you keep me so close. You simply don't want me to fail.

In faith I leave behind the mistakes and push aside things in my way.

I will conquer tomorrow by learning from yesterday.

NOW

If you are struggling with something, then you are still being disobedient. That is the bold and honest truth. It is like telling a child to clean up, and they do so by finding hidden places to put things. You can't hide anything from God, and you can't always hide things from others. Luke 6:46 says, "Why do you call me "Lord, Lord," and not do what I tell you?" Ask God to show you things keeping you from your destiny. You can't live the same old way and expect miracles.

THEN

The more I tried to change for the better, the more of a challenge it became. People I needed to cut off would just pop up. Money I thought I was saving - disappeared. Jobs I had would end and it was hard to get a new job. When I got inspired to do creative things, I could not concentrate. When I needed energy, I got very sick. When you try to do right, it seems like life wants to prove you wrong. Difficult times make us wonder if living right is worth it.

MY LESSON LEARNED

We often hear the phrase "don't put a question mark where God puts a period."

This to me means let go and move on. But there is so much more meaning to it.

I found myself in a few situations where I met the wrong people at the wrong time. And rather than recognize it and separate myself, I chose to give people the benefit of the doubt.

I believed my situation would be different because I am who I am. I wasn't judgmental, I was the one who could stick it out, be there for people, and believe what I wanted to believe.

I made excuses and I was in denial. I was wasting my time.

I mean who likes being wrong? Nobody.

But who wants to turn their back on somebody? I didn't.

We all have flaws, right.

Southern Jewel: *The Elements Within*   **by Ty A. PATTERSON**

God makes no mistakes. He created us in His image, even though we were born sinners.

We are all equal to God. If I know how to treat you, then you should know how to treat me.

Yet, there are some out there that will hang on to excuses until they leave this earth for basically ruining and sabotaging everything they touch.

They won't warn you, but God will. Once you see the writing on the wall, don't retaliate because two wrongs don't make it right.

We must stay in character. You never know who is watching you. Strong people don't have to stoop low.

Everyone has a purpose. Whether it's to teach us something, give us something, show us something, or simply listen.

We determine how long relationships last.

God also has favor.

No father wants his child to suffer.

In the same manner, you will be better off if you can recognize the wolf in sheep's clothing.

It's more than just an act of letting go and letting God.

I cannot stand unfinished business. I'd rather mend a bridge than to burn one. We seek explanations for our dilemmas when

Southern Jewel: The Elements Within   **by Ty A. PATTERSON**

the answers are in front of us.

Unfortunately, when you do get answers, you may resent what you hear and disagree, but that doesn't change a thing.

You don't have to ask a million times why, why, why?

God knows everything, and some things will be revealed to you in time.

Your inquiry gives people the impression you are focused on them. Your action leaves doors open that should be locked or burned to the ground.

God tells us "I didn't want you to have this. You need this. I want better for you. You should want better for yourself." He has even asked me, "Why carry a torch for glass that cuts you, when I want diamonds for you that make you shine?"

This is God.

This is why we should not place a question mark where God puts a period.

Be happy for every situation. Don't ask why? Just say Thanks.

Because if anything is meant to be it will work itself out.

There is nothing wrong with seeking answers, if it matters.

I am used to having things right (in my opinion) and having answers to everything. I focus too much on figuring things out that don't have a purpose, let alone an explanation.

People are going to leave you baffled many days. In my case, I have the child like attitude of proposing, "But I ain't even do nothin!" and claiming, "What you did was worse than what I did" or "but I'm the nice one."

That just leads to a revengeful heart.

Like, you just wanna' be heard so you act a damn fool all because you want answers. The sign says don't feed the monkeys for a reason. Dramatic people like disruption and chaos. Just because you don't think someone has suffered enough, doesn't mean they should.

God wants us to realize the war is over so the little battles are irrelevant. He wants us to live and enjoy tomorrow.

If you can't change the past it's ok. If you do not have all the answers, it's alright.

After all it's a recession and we are not getting paid for evaluating the past.

Whether we realize it or not, moving on is a big investment in our future. You can't change anything except yourself. Before we get side tracked and want to make things right that were wrong from the jump, let's do ourselves a favor and not do it. Pray about it, make your one attempt so your conscience is clear and drop it.

Don't Put a Question Mark Where God Puts a Period.

NOW

The elements we go through gives us a testimony. It helps knowing someone has experienced the same things we are going through. Don't you have someone you look up to? Well, that person has someone they look up to. Positive behavior is worth imitating. Galatians 6:9 says "Let us not become weary in doing good, for at the proper time we will reap a harvest if we do not give up."

THEN

We confide in everyone but the right person. There is no listening ear like God's, and He wants to hear from us. If you are going to pray don't worry, and if you're going to worry don't pray.

RESTLESS

So many sleepless nights. No one to talk to. God, you never sleep so I will talk to you.

You gave me eyes to see; you gave me ears to hear. My emotions are overflowing, and my fate is still unclear.

I know trying times are promised, but thank God for your grace. I promise to spend more time with you, and only seek your face.

Yes, I know I can't see you. But I know you are reaching out your hand. The first step to peace will be praying as you command.

I wish things didn't bother me. Sometimes I wish things would go away. It's easier said than done, you know "forgetting about yesterday."

I overthink because I am a thinker. That's one thing I cannot change but whatever is out of order in my house, I give you full authority to rearrange.

Your work is more effective than my work. Your will is what will be done. If any of my actions have caused me sleepless nights, I repent for every single one.

Southern Jewel: The Elements Within   by Ty A. PATTERSON

*You know everything about me; you made me as you felt the
need. You know what I can do without. So, do your will, I plead.*

*I know you never sleep, but I am human so I need rest. I
will take this time to pray tonight you do in my life what's best.*

*I no longer want to handle this journey. I want to be able to sit
and ride. Whatever danger is in my path, shine your lights so it
cannot hide.*

*Maybe I pick up too many people. Maybe I leave the wrong ones
behind. I give the wheel to you Lord, I just want peace of mind.*

*Am I going to the wrong places? Not knowing when mountains
are really cliffs. I am picking up trash on the side of the road
mistaking them for gifts?*

*Whatever it is, my eyes are heavy and there are no windshield
wipers for the tears. I don't trust my driving anymore, but with
you I have no fears.*

*When we reach the destination, then wake me, will you please?
Because I feel one eye closing now, and I gotta catch these zzz's.*

*I'm trusting you to get me there well rested, safe, and sound.
You have my permission to toss my needless baggage on the
ground.*

*Thanks for listening, because of you everything's alright. Prayer
was all I needed to get me through this sleepless night.*

NOW

We lose a lot of sleep trying to figure out situations God can handle. 1 Peter 4:16 says, "Yet if anyone suffers as a Christian, let him not be ashamed, but let him glorify God in that name." I tried anger, I tried laugher, I tried crying, and I tried what I thought would work. Something was still missing. I needed God. He is your earth, your fire, your water and the air in you. You have the elements within.

ABOUT THE AUTHOR

Ty A. Patterson is a published poet, the mother of two girls, and the owner of Phenomenal Gifts LLC. *Southern Jewel: The Elements Within* is her first book.

Miss Patterson was born Tykie Aushemone Tylesheon Patterson on Ft. Benning U.S. Army base in Georgia. She grew up in Center, Mississippi on the outskirts of Kosciusko not too far from the birthplaces of Television Personality, Oprah Winfrey and Civil Rights icon, James H. Meredith. Meredith's mother, Roxie, was Patterson's great aunt known affectionately as "Aunt Sis."

During high school, Patterson was active in the arts as well as Salutatorian in Literature. She previously attended Mississippi State University, Jackson State University, and holds a masters' degree from Ashford University. Patterson resides in Jackson, Mississippi where she sponsors Breast Cancer, Anti-violence, Alzheimers, and Lupus awareness activities.

Order Meredith *Etc* Titles:

www.meredithetc.com (blog)

Southern Jewel: The Elements Within by Ty A. Patterson

Starkishia: Estrella by Starkishia

Odyssey by Meredith Coleman McGee

Reverse Guilty Plea by William Trest, Jr.

Social Change and Christianity (forthcoming Jan 2015) by Dr. Rev. Louis Hathorn, Jr.

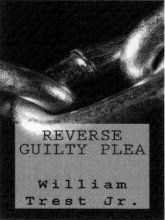

Everyone has a purpose. Whether it's to teach us something, give us something, show us something, or simply listen.

Poet Ty A. Patterson

I will conquer tomorrow by learning from yesterday.

Poet Ty A. Patterson